Unless otherwise indicated,
all scriptures references are from
International Children Bible (ICB)

**Mommy, Daddy, What Are They Doing?
Teach Your Child to Worship God**

ISBN: 978-1-953526-21-2
Copyright © November 2021
Frizelia Taylor
Jacksonville, FL, USA

All rights reserved under international copyright law. Contents and/or cover may not be reproduced in whole or part in any form without the express written consent of the publisher.
For additional copies, please visit our website:
www.taylormadepublishingfl.com
904-323-1334

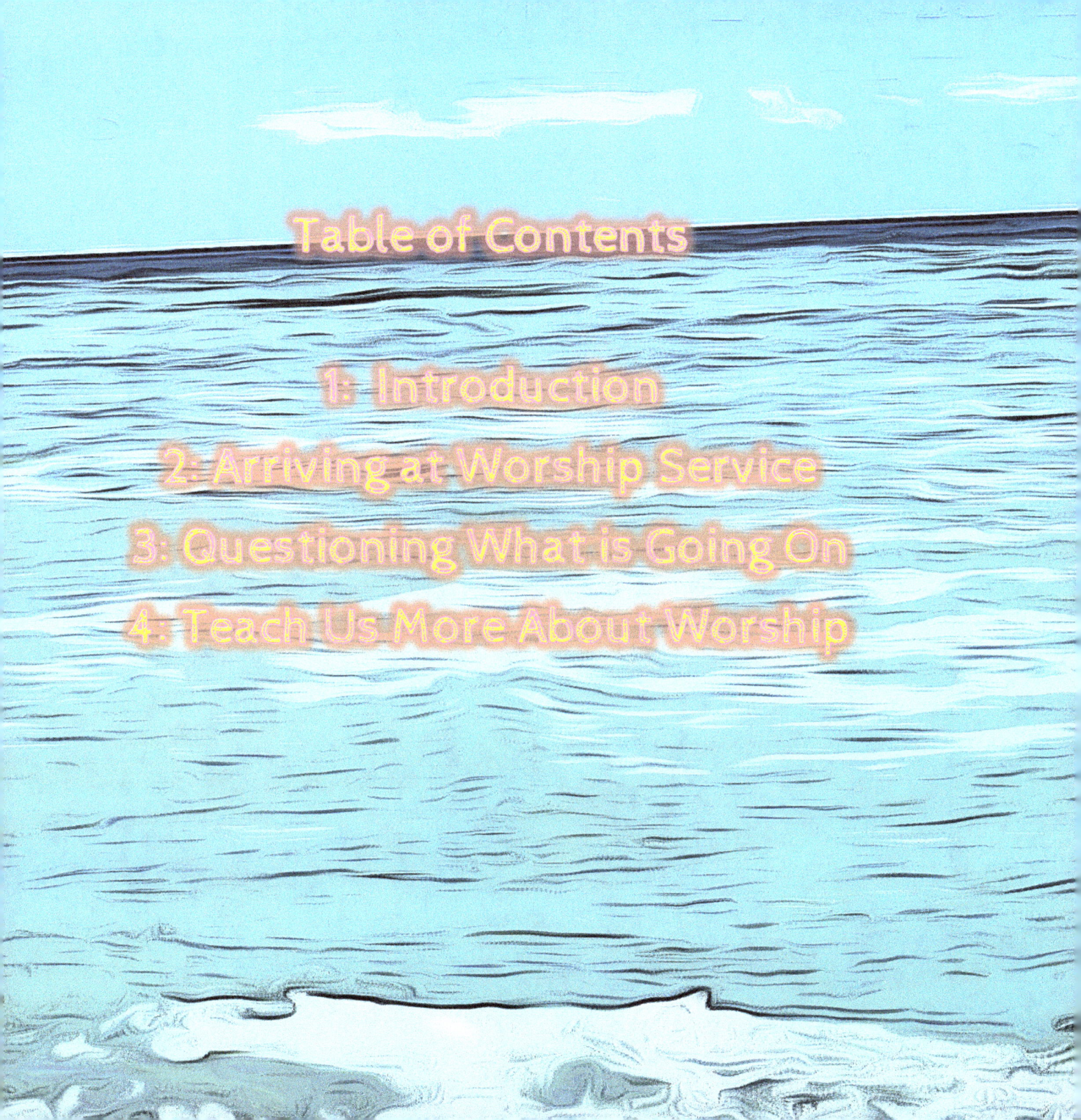

Table of Contents

1. Introduction
2. Arriving at Worship Service
3. Questioning What is Going On
4. Teach Us More About Worship

The band is playing, people were finding their way to their seats. The Miller's found four empty seats together and sat down.

Vesta spotted a family from his neighborhood, the Taylor's and their grand kids, Cliff and Fiona.

They waved at each other as Vesta headed back to his seat.

Vesta leaned over to Dyamond and said, "There are a lot of people in here!"

Dyamond said, "Yes, it is and the music is loud, but I like it!"

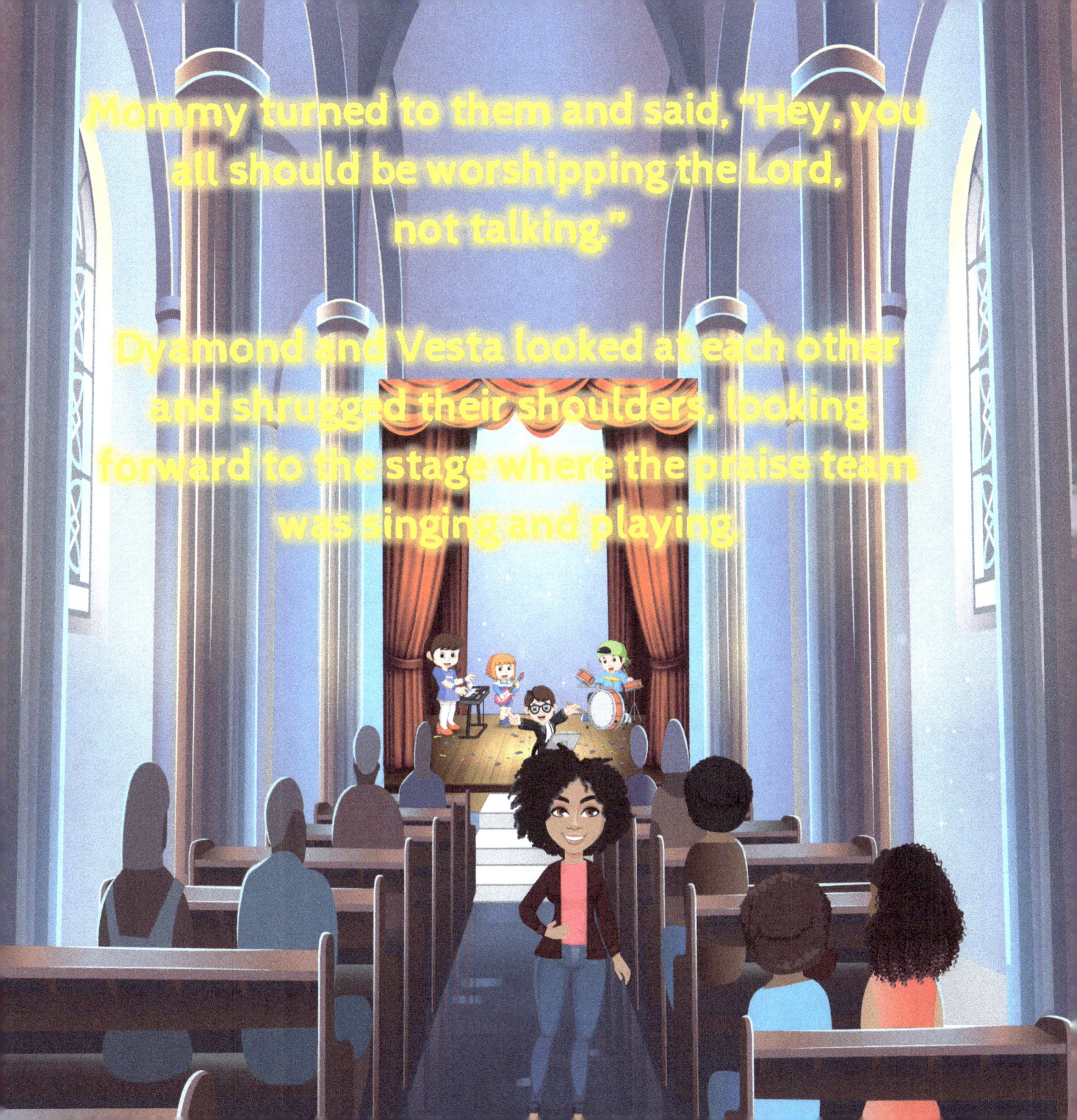

Mommy turned to them and said, "Hey, you all should be worshipping the Lord, not talking."

Dyamond and Vesta looked at each other and shrugged their shoulders, looking forward to the stage where the praise team was singing and playing.

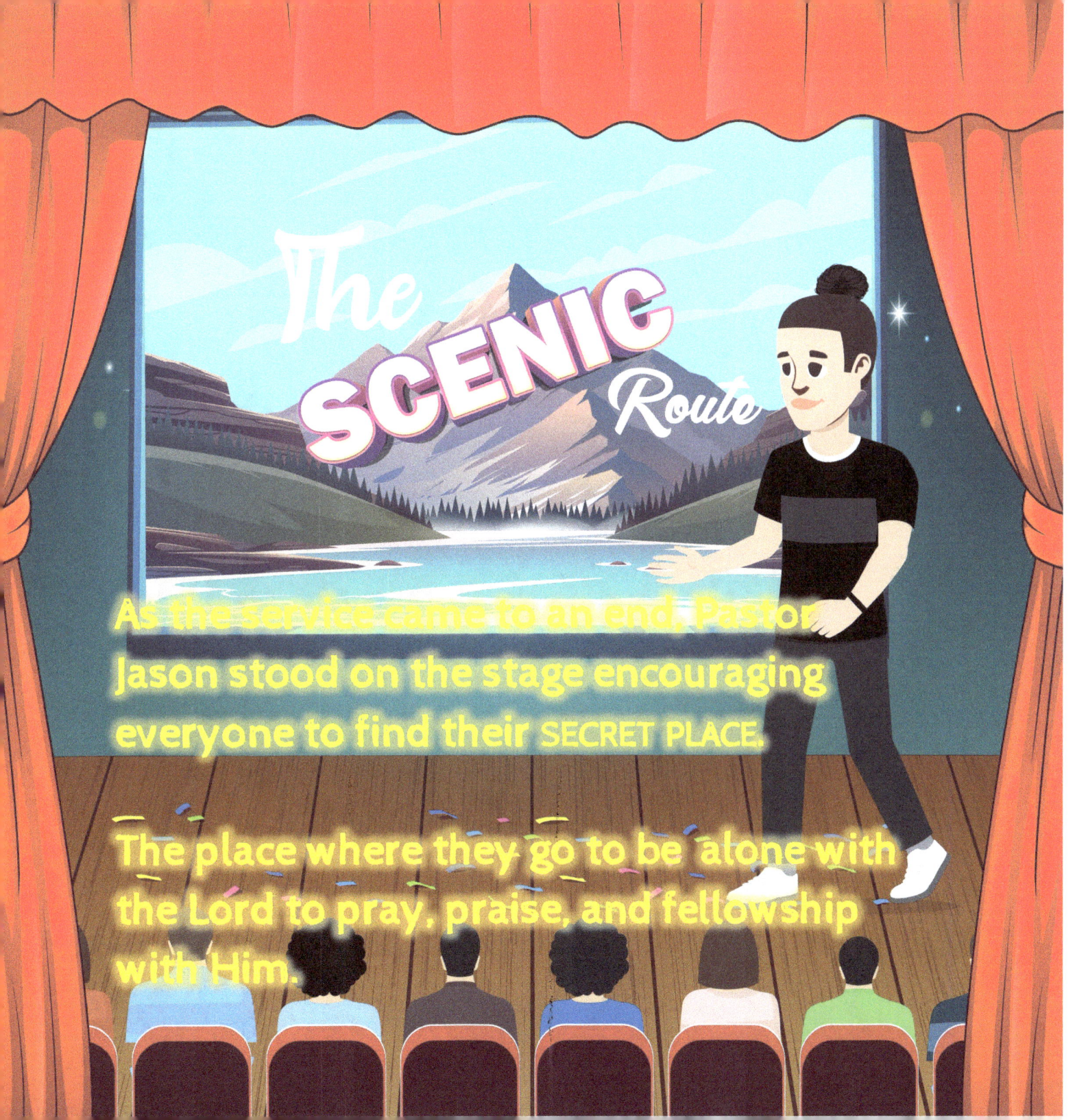

When you get in this SECRET PLACE with God, He will tell you all about the hidden treasurers.

Then, you will know for certain He is the Lord God and He called you by your name today."

Daddy said, "You go there when you pray and read your Bible in a quiet place – like your bedroom."

Vesta said, "Oh…I get it now, MY SECRET place is my prayer time like when I get up I the morning."

Dyamond said, "And before we go to bed at night." Daddy, said, Yes, you got it!"

Dyamond said, "Mommy, can you and daddy teach us more about worshipping God?"

Mommy said, "Absolutely we can teach you all more. But first, let's learn how to praise God. Let's read Psalms 100.

1 Shout to the Lord, all the earth.
2 Serve the Lord with joy.
Come before him with singing.
3 Know that the Lord is God.
He made us, and we belong to him.
We are his people, the sheep he tends.
4 Come into his city with songs of thanksgiving.
Come into his courtyards with songs of praise.
Thank him, and praise his name.
5 The Lord is good. His love continues forever.
His loyalty continues from now on.

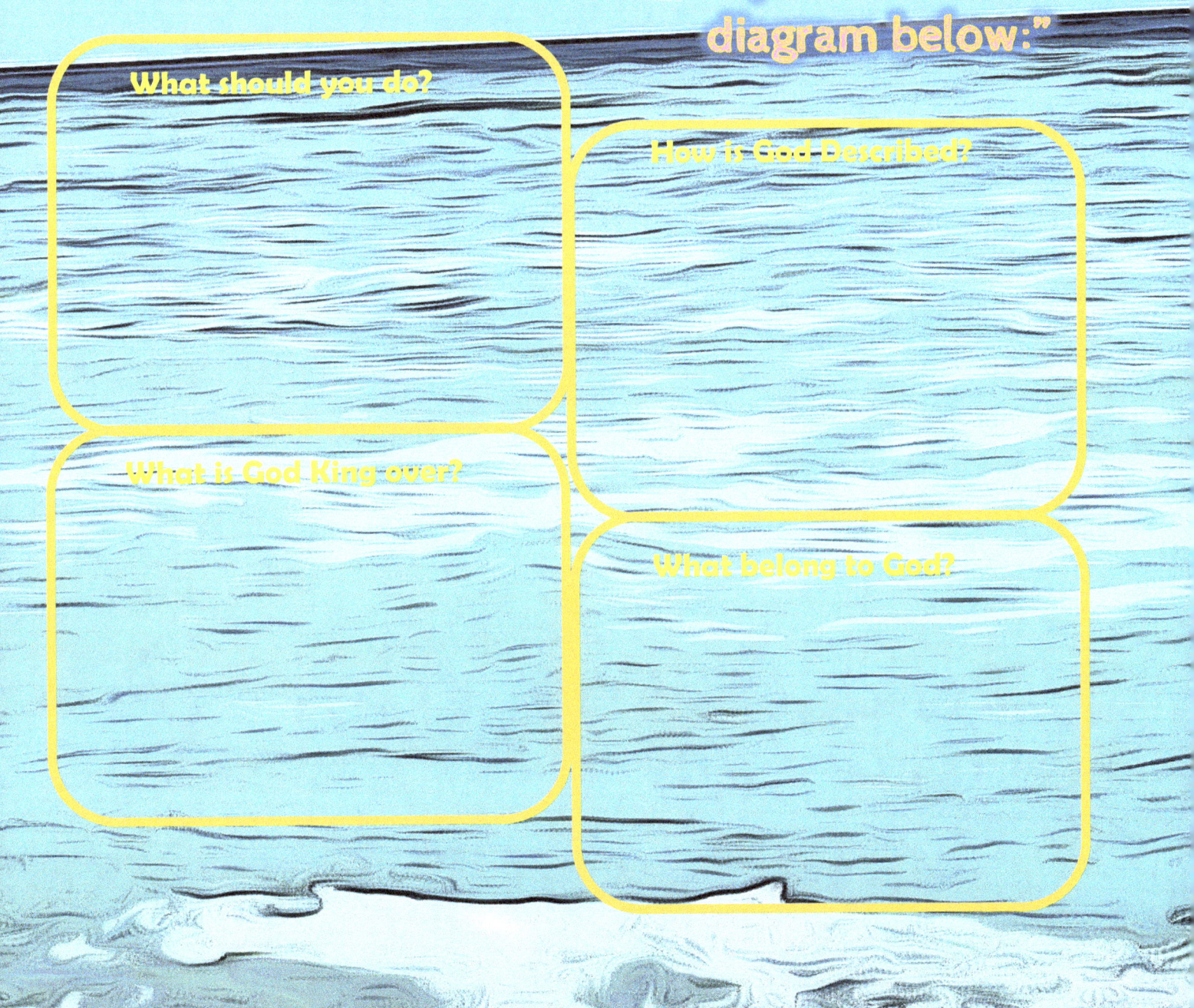

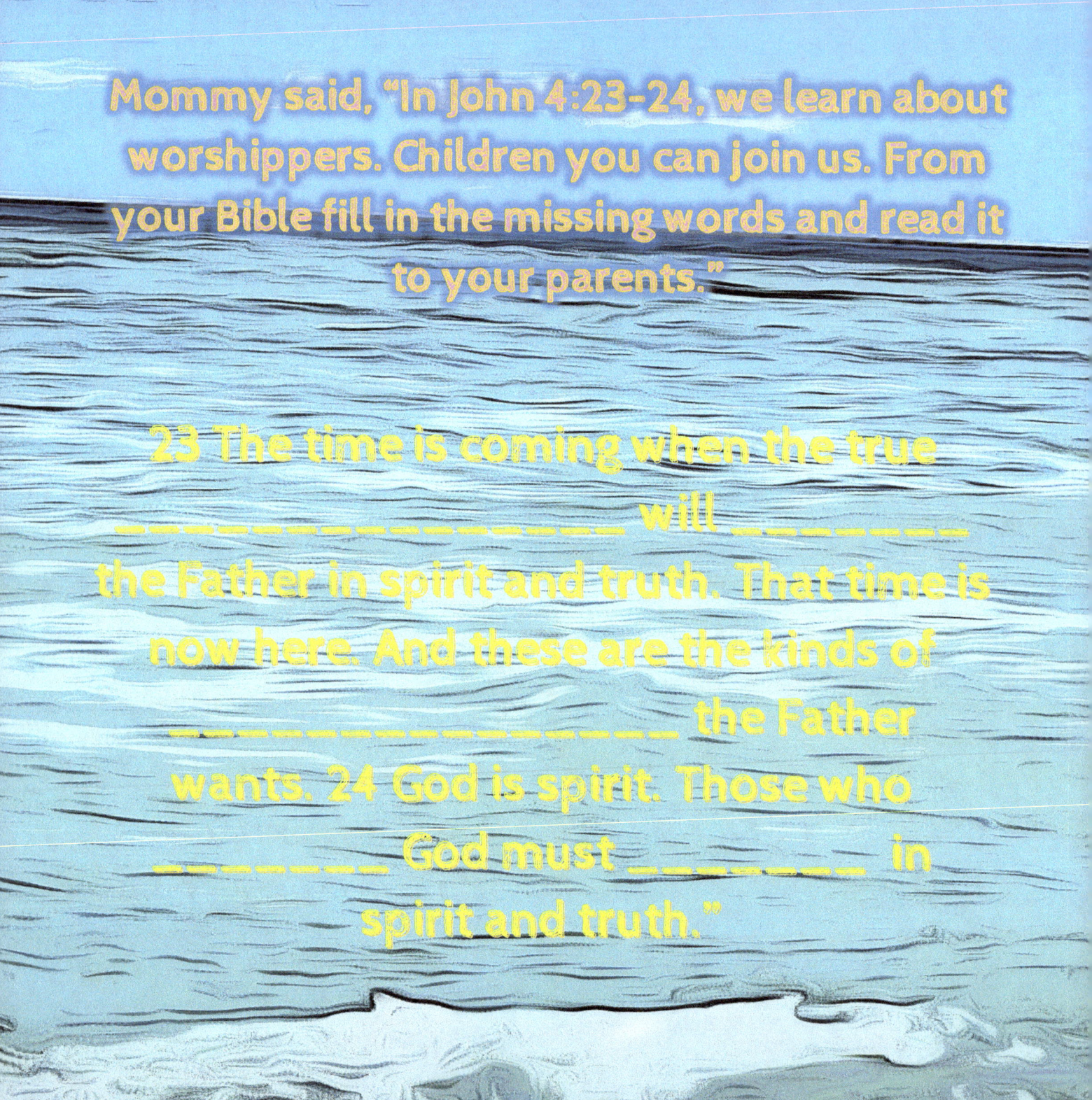

Mommy said, "In John 4:23-24, we learn about worshippers. Children you can join us. From your Bible fill in the missing words and read it to your parents."

23 The time is coming when the true _____ will _____ the Father in spirit and truth. That time is now here. And these are the kinds of _____ the Father wants. 24 God is spirit. Those who _____ God must _____ in spirit and truth."

Prayer for Children

Father, I pray for each child reading this book.
May you bless them in the journey to know You.
Teach them Lord, how to worship You. Teach them
how to honor You and put You first in their lives.
I pray for their minds to comprehend everything
they read in both the Bible and in school.
I pray Psalm 22:6 over them, they are trained
in Your ways and as they grow older they
will not depart from You.
I pray Luke 18:16 over them, they are allowed
to come Jesus and make Him Lord of their
lives and advance the Kingdom of God.
In Jesus name, amen.

Children Books by Frizella

Mommy, Who You Talking To?

Teach Your Child to Pray

Children are just as interested in praying to God as adults. In this first "Mommy" book, you will assist your child in learning how to understand and write prayers.

They will discover two other very important activities that will assist in their continuous spiritual growth in prayer:

1) They are to pray to God
2) God will hear their prayers.

ISBN: 978-1-953526-00-7

ww.taylormadepublishingfl.com

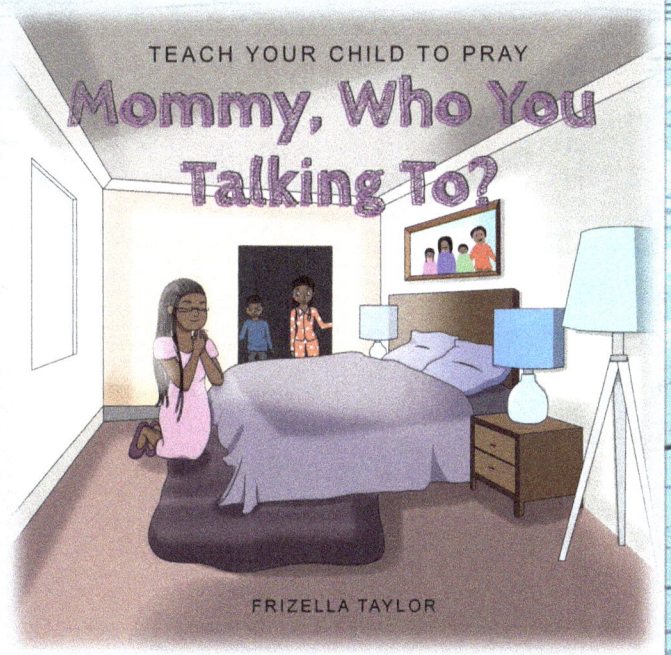

Daddy, What You Reading?

Teach Your Child to Study The Bible

Do your children know how to study the Bible? Did you know they are very capable of studying the Bible? With a little direction, they will be well on their way. Your child can learn to study the Bible.

This book will assist your child in learning how, to not just read the Bible, but actually study it. They will discover the difference between reading the Bible and studying the Bible. They will learn how to discover biblical lessons and how to apply them to their life.

Enjoy this book with your children as they glean lessons from the characters, Dyamond and Vesta; and insight and knowledge from their dad.

ISBN: 978-1-95366526-09-0

www.taylormadepublishingfl.com

www.ingramcontent.com/pod-product-compliance
Lightning Source LLC
Chambersburg PA
CBHW082041080526
44578CB00009B/796